I0478428

ISBN-13:
978-1546878407

ISBN-10:
1546878408

www.writtenmiss.com
For quantity orders, please email info@writtenmiss.com

Disclaimer

The author does not endorse individual vendors, products, or services. Therefore, any reference herein to any vendor, product, or service by trade name, trademark, manufacturer, or otherwise does not constitute or imply the author's endorsement, recommendation, or approval. All trademarks cited in this publication are the property of their respective owners. The author is in no way endorsed, sponsored, approved by, or otherwise affiliated with the owners of such trademarks.

Table of Contents

Dedication

The journey to finish this book has been quite different from my first book…stop…go…keep going. Through every step, my husband has encouraged me and I thank you, Vernon.

My other inspiration has been my sons, Michael and Matthew. May the world bless each of you with wisdom and happiness.

Acknowledgements

I want to thank the incredibly supportive group of writers at Self-Publishing School, but especially Chandler Bolt for coming up with this awesome program and Sean Sumner for holding this incredibly diverse group of people together.

Special kudos go out to my writing buddy, Lisa Love, for weekly encouragement and my writing friends, Cassandra Gaisford and R. J. Vickers.

About the Author

Marcia E. Kelley has been writing since she was six. She went on to get two Bachelor's degrees from the University of Kansas in Journalism and in English.

Marcia E. Kelley got inspiration at an early age from Alice in Wonderland. Her work experience as a Technical Writer has led her to do research on many different topics in a variety of industries.

Her two sons are in college so she knows firsthand how expensive college can be. She is married and lives in Dallas, Texas.

Introduction

Whether you are a high school student, college student, in a career, in the military or approaching retirement, there always seems to be a time when you are thinking about going to college to get a degree, add new skills or change a career. Let's face it…you may not have any money saved that you can tap immediately to take that step.

Contrary to popular belief, you can get through college without student loans! It's going to involve some research and, possibly, some hard decisions, but you will be glad you took the time to do it.

According to 2015 data:

> *Seven in 10 seniors (**69%**) who graduated from public and nonprofit colleges in 2014 had student loan debt, with an average of **$28,950** per borrower. Over the last decade—from 2004 to 2014—the share of graduates with debt rose modestly (from 65% to 69%) while **average debt at graduation rose at more than twice the rate of inflation**.*

> (Reed, 2015)

In the United States, students owe more than an estimated $1 trillion in student loans. (Nasiripour, 2015) The amount of debt owed in student loans can influence the decisions those graduates make as far as getting married, having children, buying homes and cars, and saving for retirement.

Navigating this maze of variables can seem like a daunting task, so many people just jump on the student loan bandwagon because it seems like the path of least resistance. Don't do that! Take the time to read and research.

If you take the time to do the research and plan your future based on that research, you will be able to avoid the many pitfalls of student loan debt.

What do you Want to Study?

Take some time to figure out what your interests are for coursework and for leisure-time activities. Where is the school located (near a city or in a small town)? What activities are offered? Will you live on campus or off? What food options are available? Will you have transportation? What about repairs for your transportation? What shopping options are available? What other things are important to you? Where do you live?

How do you sort all those questions out? Here's a resource:

http://www.keirsey.com/

This site gives you a list of questions to answer. The way you answer those questions can help you determine how suited you are for the career you are seeking.

We will look at how three people handle their dreams for more education without getting into debt.

Case Study 1: Meet Alex

Alex is a sophomore at a suburban high school. He's active in his community, volunteering for a variety of public service projects, he's a good student consistently at the top of his class and he plays basketball. Alex is not sure what he wants to major in when he attends college. In fact, he's not sure he wants to go to college right after high school.

Alex's parents want to help, but both of his parents have had major setbacks financially. His father works in the oil and gas industry and has had several layoffs. His mother has had to take unpaid leave from her job to care for Alex's grandmother who is elderly and needs considerable assistance. Alex's older brother, who went into the military after high school, is engaged and will soon be deployed overseas. All of the family's financial challenges mean that their credit is in ruins and there are no savings for Alex to tap into to go to college.

Alex has always been a very independent child so he decides he will find a way to go to college and pay for it himself. Alex decided to talk with his father about going to college.

"Hey, Dad."

"Hi, Alex. What's up?"

"Well, since I'm a sophomore in high school now, I've been thinking about college."

"That's great! I'm glad that you're thinking about that. College can open up many doors for you, but don't feel like you need to go to school right after high school. You may want to take some time to figure out what you want…a gap year. Remember, your brother took a year off after high school to travel before he signed up with the military. Your mom and I would love to help you, but with Grandma being sick and needing so much attention…"

"I know, Dad. I want to do this on my own, but I don't know where to start."

"You've always been so independent. Well, I would start with your counselor at school. What's her name? We met her at the beginning of the school year at the Teacher's Night event."

"Ms. Mansfield."

"Make an appointment with her and see what she says. I'll help you along the way anyway I can."

"Thanks, Dad."

Alex went to his room. He logged onto the school website, found Ms. Mansfield and made an appointment for the next day.

Alex walked into the Counselors Office. He was greeted by the receptionist.

"Hi, Alex, Ms. Mansfield is finishing with another student and will be out shortly. Have a seat."

"Thank you, ma'am." He picked up a Sports Illustrated magazine and thumbed through the pages for a few minutes, looking at the basketball stories.

"Alex, Ms. Mansfield can see you now."

Alex put down the magazine and headed to Ms. Mansfield's office.

"Hi, Alex, how are you? What brings you here to see me?" Ms. Mansfield gestured to an empty chair.

"Hi, Ms. Mansfield. I need to find out what I need to do to go to college."

"I can definitely help you with that. Do you know what you want to study?"

"I think something with sports medicine."

"Ok, well, how about kinesiology?" (American Kinesiology Association, 2015)

"What is kinesiology?" Alex asked.

"Simply, it's the study of body movement." Ms. Mansfield reached for a manual and started reading from it. "Careers using kinesiology include athletic trainer, strength and conditioning coach and exercise physiologist."

"I'm thinking athletic trainer or strength and conditioning coach."

"Ok, good. Why did you choose that field?

"I like sports."

She smiled. "How's your basketball skills this year?"

4

Alex straightened in his chair. "I've gotten several awards and my stats are good."

"Have you ever thought of playing on the college level?"

"No, ma'am."

"What about finances?"

"My Mom and Dad can't help because they're caring for my Grandma and my brother can't help because he's getting deployed in a few weeks."

"I see."

"I need to figure out a plan to pay for school myself."

"Ok, Alex. Let's figure out a plan. I will give you a list of tasks and you will check in with me periodically so that by the time you graduate, you will know what to do. Together we will figure out a plan that will allow you to get the education that you want at a pace that is comfortable for you. Come back tomorrow and I will have the first list of tasks ready for you."

"Yes, ma'am. Thank you."

The next day, Alex returned to the counselor's office. The receptionist greeted Alex and said, "Ms. Mansfield had to step out of the office, but she told me to give this to you."

He took the envelope. "Thank you, ma'am."

Here are the instructions to Alex:

Hi, Alex,

Please complete the following tasks. Document your findings. Come see me so we can discuss the next steps.

1. Set up a checking and savings account.
2. Choose two courses of study (primary and backup).
3. Choose five colleges:

      a.   Include address and admissions contact info.

      b.   Do they offer on-campus, hybrid, online, and intersession options?

4. Find a job or paid internship related to your field of study.
5. Find someone in the field of study to interview:
   a. Find out the things they like in the job
   b. Find out the things that are challenges
   c. Ask if you can job shadow for a day

Alex was confused about the different types of colleges, so he did some research and this is what he found:

Public versus Private College

Public College

Taxpayers subsidize public colleges, which is why they usually offer a discounted rate to students from that state.

Private schools receive their funding through private donations and contributions, hence a higher rate of tuition.

Ivy League

Ivy League schools are considered the cream of the crop, top of the heap…you get the picture. These schools are recognized worldwide. There are eight schools in the United States that are considered Ivy League:

- Harvard
- Yale
- Princeton
- University of Pennsylvania (Penn)
- Dartmouth
- Columbia (in New York)
- Brown
- Cornell

Types of Colleges

Junior College or Community College

Junior Colleges used to be two-year institutions that were lower divisions of private universities. The course credits that they offered were usually easily transferable to the associated university. Over the years, many junior colleges have evolved to be Community Colleges.

Tip: Many teachers teach at both the Community College and College or University levels. Check the faculty roster at both schools or ask your teachers if they teach at any other schools in the area.

Community College or College

A Community College usually only offers an Associate's degree and a two-year education. The College allows transfer of course credits from a Community College. The College occasionally offers associate degrees but typically offers undergraduate degree options.

Tip: It is to your advantage to obtain an Associate's degree at the Community College prior to transferring to a College or University.

College or University

A College tends to offer undergraduate degrees and may be smaller in size and enrollment of students.

A University offers undergraduate and graduate degrees and tends to be larger in size and the number of students enrolled.

Free Colleges

There are a number of free colleges across the United States. Some colleges offer free tuition to its students in exchange for working around campus in various capacities. Before I go further into this discussion, I want you to be aware that policies surrounding what constitutes "free" may change periodically, so if you are interested in a particular school, be sure to research it to make sure that it matches your expectations.

For example, Cooper Union, a private co-ed college located in New York, now offers only half of its tuition as free versus what it offered in 2012.

Other free colleges listed in a recent U.S. News and World Report article include the following:

- College of the Ozarks (Missouri)
- Berea College (Kentucky)
- Curtis Institute of Music (Pennsylvania)
- Alice Lloyd College (Kentucky)
- Webb Institute (New York)
- Deep Springs College (California)
- United States Military Academy – West Point (New York)
- United States Coast Guard Academy (Connecticut)
- United States Naval Academy – Annapolis (Maryland)
- United States Air Force Academy (Colorado)
- United States Merchant Marine Academy (New York)

(Hopkins, 2015)

Your research would not be complete if did not explore educational opportunities outside of the United States. Did you know there are 44 universities where Americans can study for free or almost free? Classes in these countries are usually taught in English. These countries include:

- Germany
- Iceland
- Norway
- Finland

As with anything, schools are constantly changing their policies, so be sure to research whether other schools have been added or deleted from this list.

(Lobosco, 2016)

Vocational, Technical and Trade Schools

These schools tend to concentrate on teaching students a skill that they can use to find gainful employment. These schools can be located in large cities or small towns. Many of these types of schools work with high schools so that the students gain a well-rounded education.

Tip: Sometimes credits obtained at these schools are not transferable to a college or university. Be sure to check if you want to transfer your credits in the future.

Here are some examples of classes taught at vocational schools:

- Horticulture
- Culinary arts
- Masonry
- Allied Health
- Automotive repair

Some technical schools offer:

- Construction technology
- Paralegal Studies
- Project Management
- Drafting Design
- Web Design Technology

Trade schools offer:

- Welding
- Electrician
- Carpentry
- Plumbing
- Farrier (Horseshoeing)

Three weeks later, Alex had completed all the tasks. He was ready to speak to Ms. Mansfield.

"Hi, Alex. I'm anxious to hear about your progress."

"My Dad helped me set up the checking and savings at his bank. They have student services."

"Great!"

"I chose kinesiology and journalism."

"Good. Why?"

"Well, kinesiology can be physically demanding at times, so if I were to get hurt or couldn't do my job, I'd want something that I could still do. I'm pretty good at writing and I enjoy it, so I was thinking journalism so I could maybe do some sports writing."

"Good thinking," Ms. Mansfield nodded with approval.

"I chose these schools and wrote down the contact information and the types of classes they offer next to them. Intersession threw me off. Can you help me with that one?"

"Sure, Alex. For many U.S. schools, intersession is an intense class that you take over a scheduled break like the break between Christmas and the start of the next semester. In other countries, it can be longer. A good rule of thumb: check with each individual school about their intersession schedule if they offer those types of classes."

"Ok. I found an internship with the local farm team. I start in a couple of weeks on weekends only for the rest of the school year and then we can work out a new schedule for the summer months."

"Excellent, Alex."

"I actually talked to two people in kinesiology and I wrote up a couple of paragraphs about each of their likes and challenges," Alex said as he handed the pages to Ms. Mansfield.

"Alex, I am very impressed. You did a great job. Now let's move on. I've written down what I want you to do next. There are two books I want you to read:

- <u>Find Your Passion and Purpose</u> by Cassandra Gaisford
- <u>College Can Wait</u> by R. J. Vickers

There's an exercise I would like for you to complete:

> Imagine you have just been cloned. You are now five people! Each one of you is going to head in a different direction. There are no constraints – money is not an issue and everywhere you want to go, they would hire you. You can get any job you want and you're going to get all the experience you want. What would each person be willing to try? Be bold. Be creative. Be yourself. Look for the themes. How could you turn your dream into a reality? What are all the possible options?
>
> (Gaisford, 2016)

Also, I want you to create a spreadsheet with the information from the five colleges you've chosen. Include the following information:

- College name, address and phone number
- Admissions contact information
- Website address
- Program Name
- Tuition (per credit hour)
- Admission deadline
- Application fee
- Letters of recommendation
- GPA requirement
- Essay requirements
- Transcript
- Resume requirement
- College endowment amount
- Other information you deem necessary

"I've written everything down for you and, as always, let me know when you have completed these tasks so we can discuss them."

"Yes, ma'am."

In his research, Alex ran across some terms he didn't recognize. Here's what he found out.

Residency Requirements

Each college has residency requirements that will determine the rate a student is charged for tuition. For example, if you live in Texas and want to go to college in Texas, and you have lived there for at least one year, you will be eligible for in-state tuition. To prove that you are eligible for in-state tuition, you may need to provide documentation such as mortgage payments, apartment lease, utility bills, a driver's license or state identification, voter registration, a birth certificate, tax returns or other applicable and requested documentation.

Alex took a summer class in the morning and then worked at the sports facility in the afternoon. He was also able to mow some lawns on the weekend to earn extra money. He put away 80% of his earnings into savings. He also reviewed the progress he had made toward setting himself up for a debt-free college education.

Tuition Types

Tuition is based on where you live, i.e., where you currently live and how long you've lived there or where you have previously lived. There are several different types of tuition including:

- In-state
- Out-of-state
- Reciprocity
- Foreign
- Special populations

In-state Tuition

In-state tuition is usually the lowest tuition rate, reserved for students in the state, attending a public college. For example, if you live in Texas, and have lived there for at least one year, you will be eligible for in-state tuition. To prove that you are eligible for in-state tuition, you may need to provide documentation such as mortgage payments, apartment lease information, utility bills, a driver's license or state identification, voter registration, a birth certificate, tax returns or other applicable and requested documentation.

Tip: Did you know that some schools even offer a lower tuition rate based on the county you live in?

If you live in the county where the school is located, you get the lowest rate. If you live in a nearby county (usually the county whose border touches the county where the college is located), you will be charged a slightly higher rate or the school may charge less for students that live in certain cities surrounding the college. Anyone outside that area will likely be charged the in-state tuition rate.

Out-of-state Tuition
Out-of-state tuition is charged to those students who live outside of the state or who have lived in the state for a short amount of time.

Reciprocity
Reciprocity agreements allow students from counties, regions or states to attend institutions in another area without incurring higher out of region or out-of-state tuition rates.

Check with your desired college to find out if they participate in any reciprocity agreements. Some agreements are specific to degree programs while other programs cover where the student's home address is located. Be sure to check the information to make sure it is the most current and up to date.

To find out more, click on
https://www.nasfaa.org/State_Regional_Tuition_Exchanges

(National Association of Student Financial Aid Administrators, 2016)

Foreign

The Foreign designation in regards to tuition can mean anyone living outside of the 50 states. Now different schools may slice and dice this in different ways such as outside the contiguous 48 states (i.e., all states except Alaska and Hawaii which may be charged a slightly higher tuition). Some schools may include or exclude U.S. territories such as Puerto Rico, U.S. Samoa, etc. Still, others may list Mexico, Canada and the rest of the world as a student with a foreign designation. Students who are in this category typically pay the highest rate of tuition.

Special Populations

The college, at its discretion, may offer a discount for students who qualify such as injured veterans, students with disabilities, employees of certain companies, etc. The discount given is also up to the college.

Cost Per Credit Hour

Cost per credit hour can help you get an idea of how much your degree will cost at your desired college. For example, if the cost per credit hour is $1,000 and the course of study you wish to pursue is 33 credit hours, then the estimated cost is $33,000 to complete that degree ($1,000x33=$33,000). However, some schools offer a discount of that rate based on the number of hours you take a semester. If you search the term cost per credit hour, a table or explanation will likely appear with the discounted rate, if one is offered. This calculation is only for tuition.

Endowment

An endowment is money or property given to the college. The endowment is used for continuing support for such items as scholarships, building a new wing to an existing building or a new building to expand the campus for a specific purpose. Pay attention to the amount of money in a college's scholarship fund. The more money in this fund means more scholarships may be available if you are eligible.

A month later, Alex met with Ms. Mansfield for a progress update.

"How's it going, Alex?" Ms. Mansfield asked.

"It's going great. There's a lot of things to think about."

"Yes, there are, Alex, but don't get discouraged. All the things that I've asked you to do will help you to make informed decisions as we move forward. Ok, let's review…did you read the books?"

"Yes, and I did the exercise with the five clones. That was pretty cool." He smiled. "And I learned that I don't have to rush right into college."

"You can go at your own pace, Alex."

They discussed the spreadsheet and Alex showed Ms. Mansfield the information he had compiled.

"Great job, Alex. I took a look at your grades and for your senior year, you qualify for an AP class and a dual credit class."

"What's AP and dual credit?"

"I want you to look that up along with IB classes. Also, find two degree plans from the colleges you've chosen and look at the classes you will need to take. Follow up with me when you are finished.

Advanced Classes

AP
Advanced Placement (AP) are higher-level classes offered to high school students. Many U.S. and Canadian colleges and universities will grant college credit and placement to those students obtaining high scores on the AP test for these subjects. For more information, go to https://apstudent.collegeboard.org/home?navid=gh-aps.

Dual Credit

High school juniors and seniors can earn both high school and college credit by taking certain classes. Check with both your high school and the colleges you plan to attend to see if dual credit courses are available.

IB

IB or International Baccalaureate classes are for high school juniors and seniors interested in international culture and enrichment. Six exams are required. Teachers must be authorized to teach these classes. Check to see if your high school offers these classes. To find out more information, go to: http://www.collegedata.com/cs/content/content_getinarticle_tmpl.jht ml?articleId=10027

Remedial Classes

Remedial classes are additional classes some students must take to make sure they are prepared for college level courses. All of us struggle with certain subjects from time to time. There is no shame in taking remedial classes to boost your skills. I struggle with advanced math. I'm the first one to admit it.

If you are not comfortable with a subject, ask for help. Get a tutor, find an online source or use a service like Khan Academy, https://www.khanacademy.org/.

Spend the extra time to learn it now so it does not affect your progress in the future.

Degree Plans

Alex has chosen five colleges in Texas so he would not have to pay out-of-state tuition. He used this website to find out more about the schools and to compare what each had to offer.

https://www.petersons.com/college-search/searchresults.aspx?q=Kinesiology%20and%20Exercise%20S cience&loc=||TX&page=3&resultsperpage=20

Chapter Summary

Alex wants to go to college, but his parents, brother, and grandmother are not able to help him financially. Alex enlists the help of his high school counselor to guide him through the steps to prepare him for a debt-free college education:

1. Set up a checking and savings account.
2. Choose two courses of study (primary and backup).
3. Choose five colleges:
   a. Include address and Admissions contact info.
   b. Do they offer on-campus, hybrid, online, and intersession options?
4. Find a job or paid internship related to your field of study.
5. Find someone in the field of study to interview.
   a. Find out the things they like in the job.
   b. Find out the things that are challenges.
   c. Ask if you can job shadow for a day.
6. Read *Find Your Passion and Purpose* by Cassandra Gaisford (do the clone exercise) and *College Can Wait* by R. J. Vickers.
7. Create a college information spreadsheet.
8. Find out if AP, Dual Credit or IB classes are offered at your high school or in your area.
9. Review your desired colleges' degree plans.
10. See what documentation is needed to satisfy each college's residency requirements.

Alex's Junior Year

At the beginning of his junior year, Alex received an email from Ms. Mansfield. She told him that two of the colleges he was interested in would be at their school the following week. She told him to dress up. She also provided the times and location for the appointments.

Colleges Visit High Schools

Colleges have representatives that visit high schools around the country. These representatives talk to students that are either interested in going to that school or talk to students whose teachers or counselors suggest the school. Students can ask questions and many receive invitations to visit the school. The University of Montana has a list of questions that can be used as a guide when talking with a college representative:

http://www.montana.edu/admissions/visit/repquestions.pdf

Campus Visits

A campus visit involves physically going to the campus. Students and parents can use this visit to discuss the distance from home, and to see the campus and the surrounding area. Be sure to check the crime statistics for the college you desire to attend.

Schedule plenty of time for your campus visit. Visit the campus during the day, and if possible, again at night. "Pay particular attention to walking trails to and from campus for lighting, bushes, dark allies and any other concerns. Drive around during the day and then take a second driving tour at night," (Kelley, 2015)

Standardized Tests

The ACT and SAT are the recognized standard tests for college admissions. Tests are offered several times during the year. Test prep courses are available for both. For more information, go to http://www.act.org/content/act/en/products-and-services/the-act/taking-the-test.html for the ACT and https://collegereadiness.collegeboard.org/sat for the SAT.

"Hi, Alex."

"Hi, Ms. Mansfield, I can't wait to tell you about everything."

"Wow, you've gotten taller. I see you got an A in your class. Great job! How did you like working in the sports facility?"

"It was awesome!" he said as he grinned from ear to ear.

"Did you get to do a variety of things so you could get a good feel about whether this would be a good career option for you?"

"Yes, the coaches gave me all kinds of stuff to do."

"And you mowed lawns too?"

"Yes, Ms. Mansfield, there's several elderly couples that live near us and they let me mow their lawns. They gave me great tips and cold lemonade too."

"How did the meeting with the colleges go?"

"They each invited me to visit their campus. I'll have to talk to my Dad and Mom about when we can do that."

"Let me know, Alex, because the school also organizes trips to some of the area colleges."

"Ok, cool. That's good to know."

"Before I give you your next set of tasks, I wanted to find out how your family is doing."

"My Dad has started getting some calls from companies. Things are picking up and he may be going back to work soon. My Mom has had to quit her job because Grandma is not doing well. My brother has been deployed overseas and won't be back for about a year."

"Good news for your Dad. I hope that works out for him. I'm sorry to hear that your Mom had to quit her job and that your Grandma is not doing well. I know you miss your brother."

"Yes, thank you, Ms. Mansfield. What are my new tasks?"

"Start looking for scholarships and apply to them. Here's the schedule for campus visits for this semester. See if any of your colleges are on the list and talk with your parents to make sure you can go. See if your parents can take you for any of the other campus visits. Let me know if you need any help."

Alex's father went back to work, so Alex was able to visit all five of his schools by the end of the semester. His father's new job offered a $1,000 scholarship so he and his father applied. He found a couple of other scholarships in the amount of $500 and $250, respectively. Alex continued to work around his class schedule at the sports facility. Just before Christmas break, he went in to talk with Ms. Mansfield.

"Hi, Alex, how are you?"

"I'm ok."

"I've been hearing good reports from all of your teachers. Why are you so sad?"

"My Grandma is in hospice."

"Oh, Alex, I'm so sorry."

Alex wiped away a tear. Ms. Mansfield handed him a tissue.

"I don't like seeing Grandma like this."

"I know it's hard, Alex. Is there anything I can do?"

Alex was quiet for a few moments. He told Ms. Mansfield about his father's job, the scholarships, and his work at the sports facility.

"Alex, you have done really well. I only have one task for you to do this time. Have your parents help you fill out the FAFSA form. Try to take some time to be with your family over the holidays. We can talk again after the break."

FAFSA

FAFSA (Free Application for Federal Student Aid, www.fafsa.gov) is an application used by all students seeking financial aid. That aid can be in the form of grants, loans, and work-study funds.

Ms. Mansfield looked outside as light snow fell on students coming back to the high school after the holiday break. Just as she picked up her coffee cup to take a drink, the familiar ping of an incoming email focused her attention on the computer screen. It was from Alex. It read, "Good morning, Ms. Mansfield, I will need to reschedule my meeting with you tomorrow. My Grandmother just passed away."

She paused, then hit Reply. "Dear Alex, my condolences to you and your family. I will let your teachers know. When things settle down, feel free to contact me."

Three weeks went by before she heard from Alex requesting a meeting.

"Hi, Alex, how are you? Come in," she said as she motioned to a nearby chair.

"Hi, Ms. Mansfield. I'm good." He fidgeted with his backpack and produced some papers. "I have applied to several more scholarships, I visited two campuses and my Dad and I are going to the other three later this month and next month. I filled out the FAFSA and I'll update it when Mom and Dad file their taxes."

She moved the papers to the side of her desk and folded her hands in front of her. "Alex, are you okay?"

"Yes, my Grandma…I didn't like seeing her suffer. She didn't deserve that. I miss her, but it's okay."

"Once again, Alex, you've done a wonderful job with all the tasks. How do you feel about all the things you have done to this point?"

"It's been really helpful. I can see why the planning is such an important step. Do you think I'll be ready for graduation next year?"

"Yes, I do. The rest of this school year, I want you to concentrate on budgeting. Be sure to include such things as housing, car and car repairs, meals, clothing and anything else you would typically need for your first two years at your most expensive school and another plan for two years at the least expensive school then transferring to your most expensive school. Build in a cushion for tuition increases and unexpected expenses. Do you know what you are going to do over the summer?"

"I'm going to work at the sports facility and mow the lawns again. I'm going to take the summer off from school. I'm going to help Mom and Dad go through Grandma's things."

"Sounds like a great plan. Don't forget to take some time for some fun activities with your friends or take up a hobby. Touch base with me before you leave for summer break."

"I will. Thank you, Ms. Mansfield."

Other Considerations

Housing

You will need to have a place to live while you are in college. The most likely options are:

- On campus
- Off campus
- At home

Tip: An estimated cost breakdown will usually include tuition, housing, meal plans, transportation, medical and miscellaneous costs.

On campus

Many universities require freshman students to live on campus in dormitories. One to four people share a dormitory that includes a sleeping area and a study area. Bathroom and shower facilities may be in the room or down the hall in a communal space. Dormitories may also be co-ed (co-educational for boys and girls) or for a single sex (either boys or girls).

Most community colleges do not have dormitories. This is another cost savings to you.

Off-Campus/At Home
Off-campus housing may include apartments, sharing a house or living with parents or relatives. This type of housing tends to be slightly less expensive than dorm life.

Refrigerator, Microwave, and Other Appliances
Institutions have strict policies about appliances allowed in dorm rooms and on college campuses. These policies are put into place for safety reasons and are updated frequently. Verify what appliances are allowed before you move.

Meal Plans
Meal plans on college campuses are varied. Some offer 1-4 meals a day (3 meals and a snack), some offer pre-packaged options for the busy student so they can grab it and go. Still, others offer national chain restaurants and others offer something similar to a home-cooked option with options for meat, vegetables, bread, and desserts.

The settings vary as well from the traditional school cafeteria setup to food stations where different types of foods are offered at each station (Asian, Italian, American, etc.). Some seem very institutional and functional with tables and chairs in a large open space, to more of a restaurant feel with tables, booths, and high-end décor.

With so many options available, it can be hard to choose. Try to leave enough time during your campus visit to try some of the food options.

Find out how often you pay for the meal plan: weekly, monthly, quarterly or annually. Also, if you have any dietary restrictions, find out if there are meal plans to accommodate your needs. You can even find out if there are options based on the size of your meal. For example, Central Washington University in Ellensburg, Washington offers athletic, large, medium, and small meal plans:

www.cwu.edu/dining/meal-plan

Groceries
Do some research and look at the cost of the meal plan versus buying food from the grocery store. There you can find fresh fruits, vegetables, and meats along with packaged frozen meals. Some stores also offer prepared meals.

Online Food Delivery
Recently, several online food services have popped up offering fresh or packaged meals, even for those students with dietary needs, delivered to your door. Some of these services offer meal plans for individuals or several people. These services also offer discounts and rewards to their customers.

www.emeals.com/

www.schwans.com/

www.hellofresh.com

www.homechef.com

www.plated.com

www.chefd.com/

www.blueapron.com/

Tip: Share the cost of these services with another student, for example. Check the availability of these services in your area.

Cooking and Storing Food

College campuses have policies in place governing items you can have in your dorm room such as microwaves, hot plates, crockpots and refrigerators. Some dormitories are equipped with microwaves so students can heat up meals.

Some institutions allow small refrigerators in dorm rooms while others only have a common area with a microwave and refrigerator available.

Transportation

Distance

How far is your desired college from your home? What type of transportation will you need to use? How much will it cost? How convenient is your transportation choice in the event you have an emergency and need to leave quickly? Consider the costs for these types of transportation:

- Airlines
- Train
- Bus
- Bike
- Motorcycle or Moped
- Car Pool
- Sharing services (Uber, Lyft)

Remember to consider service providers, safety records, how to get to them if you don't have a car of your own, and insurance (liability, trip cancellation, etc.).

Other Costs

Insurance

Homeowner's insurance may cover your belongings at home, but what type of insurance do you need for your dorm room, apartment or other housing choice away from home? Don't forget to cover your contents such as a laptop and other items.

Repairs/Maintenance

If you have a car, bike, motorcycle, or moped, you will need to have service to keep your transportation in top running condition. Who will service it? Who can you trust? Watch out for establishments who have complaints about price gouging or poor service.

Gas

Find a couple of gas stations that you trust and can give you a good price on gas. There are numerous apps to help you find gas stations in your area: Gas Buddy, Gas Guru and Waze.

Buying a Car

Look for a reliable car with decent gas mileage and low maintenance costs. There are several great car buying services online such as www.cars.com, www.truecar.com and www.carvana.com.

For peace of mind, look at the ratings for local dealers on the Better Business Bureau website at www.bbb.com.

Clothing

There are so many options for clothing that didn't exist even two years ago.

Rent

You've been invited to a party or you have an interview with a company and you want to buy something new but don't have the funds? Why not rent?

Rent a tux, an evening gown, a suit, shoes, coat…just about anything you can think of, you can rent.

Here are some suggestions:

- www.blacktux.com
- www.renttherunway.com/

Buy

Shopping models are changing, especially when you are talking about online services. There are shopping sites that take orders for a few days then buy in bulk and ship the orders to you like www.zulily.com.

Other sites offer clothing at wholesale prices for men's and women's clothing such as www.rosewholesale.com, www.sammydress.com and www.lightinthebox.com/ for men only.

Consignment

Consignment shops tend to cater to customers wanting high-end designer clothing and accessories. Each consignment shop sets its own policies. Most consignment stores allow you to bring your items to the store for a set period of time. Each item is tagged with a special identifier so that you will get credit when the item sells. If the items do not sell during the designated time period, the shop can either ask you to pick up the items or reduce the price. The store takes a commission from the sale of your items.

Online clothing consignment shops are starting to pop up such as:

www.swap.com

www.thredup.com

www.schoola.com

Consignment shops for furniture, bicycles, and other items are gaining popularity.

Tip: Before agreeing to any Consignment Agreement, make sure to read the fine print and know all the terms and conditions involved.

Thrift Stores

Thrift stores operate primarily on donations and are usually tied to a non-profit organization. The sale of donated items support services of the non-profit. Donors get a receipt which they can use for a tax deduction.

Some examples of thrift stores include the Salvation Army and Goodwill.

Books

Textbooks for classes can run the gamut from cheap to very expensive. Books can come in hardcover or paperback and some schools are even allowing ebooks for students.

Students can buy or rent books for their classes, but what do you do with your books at the end of the semester? Most students sell them back. Students can use the on-campus buyback program, used bookstores, or online options:

www.amazon.com

www.bookbyte.com

www.chegg.com/

Tip: Ebooks require an ebook reader such as a Kindle (Amazon) or Nook (Barnes and Noble) or ereader software application.

Medical

Hospital

Students should locate medical services and facilities during their campus visit. Find out what services are provided and the location of nearby hospitals if the student needs to be transported to another facility.

Insurance

Review your medical insurance to find out if your current coverage is sufficient or if you need to make changes based on coverage limits or location.

Hobbies

A hobby is something that you do for fun such as playing sports, collecting items, doing crafty and creative projects. Here are some ideas:

- Sports (tennis, golf, bowling, archery, etc.)
- Collecting items (stamps, baseball cards, antiques, etc.)
- Crafts/creative (quilting, needlework, soap making, drawing/painting, etc.)

Chapter Summary

Alex has made significant progress in planning his path to a debt-free college education.

1. Alex met with two college representatives that visited his high school.
2. Alex and his Dad visited two college campuses and have three more visits scheduled.
3. Alex continued looking for scholarships.
4. He and his Dad filled out the FAFSA form.
5. He is budgeting for all expenses for the first two years of college.

6. He will be working at the sports facility, mowing lawns and helping his family with his Grandmother's belongings.

Alex's Senior Year

Summer passed far too quickly and Alex walked back into high school as a senior. He had a great summer and was anxious to speak with Ms. Mansfield.

"Hi, Ms. Mansfield. I have so much to tell you."

"Hi, Alex. I take it you had a great summer."

"I got a scholarship! Remember, I told you that my Dad's new job had a scholarship? I got it!"

"That's wonderful, Alex. Was that the one for $1,000?"

"Yes, and it's renewable for up to 4 years! I did my budgeting and I have enough for two years at my lowest priced college and then transfer to my university for the last two years. But I still have some more scholarship applications out there that I haven't heard from yet and another summer before school starts."

"That's right and you need to apply to colleges this year. They may offer additional scholarships and grants, Alex."

"Oh, and I forgot to tell you a couple of other things."

"What?"

"I was voted MVP for the basketball team and I will be team captain this year. Coach says I might get a Letter of Intent from one of the colleges. Also, my Grandma left me $2,500."

"That's awesome! You have had a great summer."

"Yes, Ms. Mansfield, what do I need to do this semester?"

"Get more information on the Letter of Intent process at http://www.nationalletter.org/. Be sure to review all your colleges to find out when the applications are due. They will probably be between November and March depending on whether they are early, regular, or late deadlines. Go for early application deadlines and find out if they will notify you online or by mail. Also, see if you can apply to multiple colleges with a common application.

Check whether you qualify for a fee waiver for the application fees. Talk to your English teacher about college essays."

"Ok, got it."

"Be sure to contact me if you have any questions."

"I will. Gotta run or I'll be late for class. Thank you, Ms. Mansfield."

Tip: High school seniors can also check out http://www.collegesimply.com/guides/application-deadlines/ for college application deadlines.

Types of Scholarships

Renewable Scholarships
Renewable scholarships are ones that can be used for a set time period, for example, four years. There are usually eligibility requirements attached to the renewability such as maintaining a certain GPA (Grade Point Average), attending a certain institution, or other restrictions.

Athletic Scholarships
These scholarships are awarded to student athletes in a particular sport such as football or basketball, but they may be available for additional sports such as golf, lacrosse, tennis and more. These scholarships may be designated for one school, a group of schools or it may have other restrictions. If a student receives this type of scholarship, be aware of restrictions, clauses and other language associated with this type of scholarship. Also, the athlete should know what his/her options are in the event of an injury or illness that could impact his/her ability to play.

Academic Scholarships

This type of scholarship is awarded to students that excel in activities other than sports and that have a certain GPA. Sometimes called a "merit-based" scholarship, this scholarship can also be awarded for standardized test score excellence, from private sources organizations or from the student's intended institution.

Grants

Grants and scholarships are frequently confused. Neither require the recipient to pay back these monies. Grants are monies given to someone based on a need and scholarships are usually tied to academic or merit recognition such as good grades, GPA, etc. (The College Board, 2016)

Work Study

Work Study is a federally funded program that allows students to work while attending college. The program is meant to help students with the costs of their education by working part-time. The program is based on need and the student must meet certain eligibility requirements.

Tip: You may be able to request additional funds or negotiate a larger amount. Your request can be approved or denied.

Financial Aid Package

The financial aid package can include loans, grants, and scholarships from multiple sources to help you pay for college costs. You must notify the school of your decision to accept or decline what is awarded to you.

College Applications

Review all information from your desired institutions regarding how to apply for admission. Some colleges will only accept the application from their institution, while other colleges will accept a Common Application.

Common Application

This application is used to apply to multiple colleges at once. The advantages of using a Common Application is that you only need to fill out an application once; the disadvantage is that the essay included must be generic enough to use for all the colleges to which you are applying.

For more information, go to https://www.commonapp.org/.

Tip: Read all application instructions thoroughly to make sure everything is complete. Incomplete applications may be rejected.

Alex made an appointment to see Ms. Mansfield before the holiday break.

"Hi, Ms. Mansfield."

"Hi, Alex."

"My English teacher reviewed my essay and helped me to polish it. I was able to apply to four of my schools with the Common Application and was able to get a fee reduction. I applied over Thanksgiving break. I will apply to the last college by January 1."

"Ok, Alex, now the nail-biting begins. When will you have a decision from each of the schools?"

"I should have all decisions by the end of January."

"Come and see me when you get the decisions. This is very exciting, Alex."

"Thank you, Ms. Mansfield."

College Decisions

Over the next month, Alex got decision letters from all five institutions. He couldn't wait to tell Ms. Mansfield.

"Ok, Alex, give me the good news," Ms. Mansfield said.

"I got accepted into four and denied by one." They looked at the letters together. Two of the colleges offered a combination of student loans, scholarships, and grants. One offered a partial athletic scholarship, a partial academic scholarship, and a grant and the last school offered to cover tuition only. The denial was Alex's number one college.

"Let's eliminate the two that have the student loans because the loans are very high for the four years."

"Agreed. Talk with your parents and let me know what you decide."

"I have to let both colleges know by the end of March. Right now, I'm going to concentrate on the state basketball tournament."

"Yes, February is a busy month. Good luck at State!"

A week later, Ms. Mansfield was at home watching the highlights from the state's basketball tournament on the news. She dropped her bowl of popcorn on the floor. "Oh, no!"

The following week, Alex came to her office on crutches and slumped into a chair in her office.

"Hi, Alex."

"It all happened so fast. I went up for a shot, but when I landed, I stepped down wrong and got hit by one of the other players."

"How bad is it?"

"I broke my tibia. It was a compound fracture. I've already had a rod inserted, but it will probably be at least a year before I can play again. That means I won't be able to play next season."

"I just saw that you were hurt on the news. I didn't know how bad it was. I'm so sorry, Alex."

"Since I'm going to need quite a bit of rehab, I need to stay close to my doctors, so that may impact my college decision."

"Yes, it may. Call your colleges. Set up an appointment to meet with them in person. Explain your situation. Ask about a possible deferment. Choose an option that works for your situation. Also, ask if there are any College Placement Tests you can take. Let me know what you decide."

"I will. Thank you, Ms. Mansfield."

Deferment

Deferment, sometimes called deferral, happens when circumstances occur that make it necessary for the student to change their plans for when they will start college. Here are some acceptable reasons:

- Wanting a gap year between high school and starting college
- Serious illness or injury to the student or the student's immediate family

Talk about how deferment can affect your financial aid package. To find out more, visit http://www.princetonreview.com/college-advice/deferred-admission.

Reduction in Hours

Talk with the college about reducing the number of hours you will attend. You may be able to reduce your status to a part-time student status to retain or only slightly reduce your financial aid package.

About a month later, Ms. Mansfield sent an invitation to Alex to attend the Senior Awards Ceremony. This is a ceremony where seniors find out if they have received additional scholarships and other awards such as honors achievements and attendance awards.

Alex received a $1,000 scholarship from an organization for his public service, working with underprivileged children.

He also scheduled to take the College Placement Tests.

College Placement Tests

Colleges use College Placement Tests to check the skills of students in math and writing. Some schools also use similar tests to gauge the proficiency with foreign languages. The tests can help with placing a student in a remedial or higher level class or to test out of a subject. For more information, go to https://bigfuture.collegeboard.org/find-colleges/academic-life/what-are-college-placement-tests.

A few days later, Ms. Mansfield walked into her office and noticed two sealed envelopes on her desk. One was an invitation to Alex's graduation ceremony and the other was a hand-written thank you note:

Dear Ms. Mansfield,

Graduation Day is almost here. It's my first life milestone. I am so glad that you helped me to walk this path with confidence. I won't let you down.

Thank you.

Alex

Graduation Day

The students filed into the auditorium as the graduation music played. Ms. Mansfield sat quietly as each student's name was read. She sat up in her seat as the announcer read Alex's name. She gave him a thumbs up signal.

After the ceremony was over, the parents, students, and teachers mingled while enjoying cake and punch. Alex, with his parents in tow, found Ms. Mansfield talking with the principal.

"Ms. Mansfield, you remember my parents?" Alex introduced his parents to his teacher.

"How are you? You must be so proud of Alex."

"Yes, we are," Alex's mother said.

"I know that it's been a tough couple of years for the entire family."

"Yes, it has been, but things are looking up. I'm starting a new job next week." Alex's mother smiled.

"And I just got a promotion," Alex's father chimed in.

"I just got a letter today saying the college will defer my start date for a year. I'm going to go to summer school at the smaller school this summer and next summer and will take a full load during the year. With the AP class I took, and 9 hours of dual credit, that will count toward my credits. And I was able to test out of the math requirement."

"Great job, Alex. Good luck in everything you do going forward. Drop me an email occasionally to let me know how you are doing."

"I will. Thank you so much, Ms. Mansfield."

With that, Alex and his parents left.

Case Study 2: James

James is a hard worker. He started with this company shortly after graduating from high school. Over the last 21 years, he's managed to get some promotions and has been recognized with bonuses for his hard work.

There's been rumors that another company wants to buy this company. James is worried about his job prospects since he never went to college. He's worried about taking care of his wife and three small children, aged 6, 4, and 2.

The Layoff

On Friday, his boss calls James into his office.

"James, I know you've heard the rumors about how we might be bought out. I wanted to let you know that they are looking at employees that have been with us for over 20 years. They are offering an early out package."

"Do you mean they're going to let me go?" James couldn't hide the panic in his voice.

"Yes, but you're still a young man. You would be eligible for two weeks' pay for each year, a bonus of an additional two months' pay because of your current position, tuition assistance for four years, and medical coverage for you for four years. You will need to pay to cover your family. You can go to college or vo-tech and train for something new. Go down to Human Resources and they'll have the paperwork for you."

And just like that, James was let go. His wife, Emily, had planned a 40th birthday party for him for that evening. He drove home in silence. He decided to leave the paperwork in the car and pretend that everything was fine until after the party was over.

When he walked in the door, people jumped out from their hiding places and yelled "Surprise!" A tear rolled down James's cheek.

Most people thought it was because he was glad to see them. His wife knew better but she played along until everyone was gone.

"Honey, what's wrong? Are you upset at turning 40? You know 40 is the new…"

"I got laid off today."

She hugged him tight and kissed him gently. "We'll be alright, honey. Why don't you just relax for a few days and figure out what you want to do."

James took his wife's advice. He took a couple weeks to think about what he wanted to do and what his new life would look like. He took long walks around a nearby park. He played with his kids. He took a long drive to a lake and state park. He even planned a weekend trip with his family.

My New Life

James woke up a different man. He pulled up a chair at breakfast and announced to his wife, "Today, I start my new life."

James spent the morning on the computer doing research and humming along to his favorite songs playing through his earphones. At noon, he stopped to share lunch with his wife and his younger two children.

"I've set up an appointment with a financial planner and a career coach for this week."

"That's great, honey."

"I want you to know that I'm doing everything in my power to take care of you and the kids," James quickly kissed his wife and headed back to the computer.

James took the advice of the financial planner and set up investment accounts that would secure his family's future. He also met with the career coach to discuss some possible career options going forward. He shared the information of both appointments with his wife.

"Emily, can you come here? I want to show you the investment plan for us going forward." James sat down with his wife at the computer and he went over what he and the financial planner had discussed. Their discussion was interrupted by the sounds of crying from the playroom. They both jumped up and ran to see what their 2 and 4 year olds were doing. The 4 year old, Jay, had taken a favorite toy from their 2 year old, Maggie. They each comforted a child and then turned on a TV show that both children loved.

"Ok, crisis averted," Emily sighed.

"Yes," James agreed. They shared a laugh.

"So how did the appointment with the career coach go?" Emily asked.

"It went great. She gave me a couple of assessment tests to help me figure out what my personality type is and what types of jobs I may be good at."

"I could have done that for you," Emily gave James a playful punch to his shoulder. "You are a very caring person and you like helping people."

"You're right, but she helped me to look at some careers that might work for me."

"Ok, what did she suggest, or better yet, what do you feel you would like to do?"

"I think I want to do something in healthcare," James said.

"Like what?"

"I think I want to be a nurse." Emily was a bit surprised.

"Really?"

"Yeah, it feels right. I want to help people."

"Does anything about that scare you, like, the blood, death...are you sure about that?"

"I'm sure. We looked at several schools. I've chosen this one." He pointed to a brochure laying on his desk. "And classes start in two weeks."

"Wow! That's great, honey." Emily gave James a big hug. "I'm so proud of you."

James used his tuition assistance from his former position to take care of the tuition and books. He was able to get a discount on a stethoscope, comfortable shoes, scrubs and other supplies that he needed because he was a displaced worker.

Tuition Assistance

Some employers offer tuition assistance to their employees. In many cases, the employee will pay the tuition and get the books for the class. At the end of the class, if the employee passes the class, the employer will then reimburse the employee for the amount of the tuition and books. If the employee does not pass with the required grade, the employer may give the employee partial reimbursement or no reimbursement at all depending on the company policy.

Additionally, some employers will only pay for classes related to the employee's current job. For example, if the employee is a technician in the IT (Information Technology) department, he/she may only be authorized to take classes related to IT. Other employers may pay for any college level classes.

Tip: Smart employees will take the money that is given to them from one semester and roll that amount into future semesters, effectively going to school without any further, or only minimal, out-of-pocket expenses.

Be sure to check with the appropriate representatives at the school (usually in the Financial Aid Office) and at the employer (usually Human Resources) to make sure that you are taking classes for which you can be reimbursed. In addition, if you leave the company, you may need to pay back some or all of the assistance you gained while you were employed. (Dumbauld, 2016)

Displaced Worker

A displaced worker can be anyone who has lost their job because there was insufficient work, the location closed or moved, the position was eliminated or may even apply to some military positions.

Tip: Check with your local unemployment office to see if you qualify for displaced worker status and if any additional services are available to you.

Chapter Summary

James was given lemons when he lost his job of 21 years. He didn't know what to do, but his former company was very generous providing severance, tuition assistance, and healthcare. This was the only job he had ever known.

James took some time to clear his head. He talked to a financial planner and a career coach and researched possible new careers.

He was able to determine that he wanted a career where he could help others. He decided on nursing, a career that could give him rewards and an income greater than what he had left.

Case Study 3: Muriel

Muriel is 58, widowed, and the mother of two grown children. She was a stay-at-home Mom until her world was turned upside down. Her husband of 17 years was killed on an ice-covered road on his way home from work. Her children, Abby and Cole, were 10 and 11 at the time. The family had been struggling financially after his hours were cut at the manufacturing plant where he worked. His company provided a life insurance policy that covered his burial expenses and Muriel was able to pay off some bills, but she quickly realized that she would have to go to work to keep her family afloat.

She had substituted at her children's elementary school in the classroom and filled in for vacations at the front office. Muriel had managed to take some classes at the local community college over the years, but needed to transfer to the local university to get her Bachelor's degree.

She talked with her school's admissions office and the university's admissions office to find out what credits would transfer. She then contacted her financial planner and came up with a plan to go to school full-time for the summer and fall semester. After that, she would need to find full-time work to support the family and go to school at night to finish her degree.

Muriel dived in her classes taking time out to spend time with Abby and Cole. Over time, the sadness turned to fond memories of their father and the time they now spent with their mother. In early November, Muriel got a phone call from one of the teachers at the elementary school where she used to work.

"Hi, Muriel, how are you?"

"I'm fine and you?"

"I'm great. How are Abby and Cole?"

"They're doing pretty good. They miss their father."

"Of course. Muriel, I called to let you know that one of my friends at the university is moving. Her husband's job is transferring him to the East Coast in January. I wanted to let you know because she will be leaving and the position would be perfect for you."

Muriel jotted down some notes and watched for the position on the university's website. She applied and two weeks later, found herself interviewing for the position. Three days after that, she received a call offering her the job. She quickly accepted. She felt like a weight had been lifted off her shoulders. She nearly danced through the aisles at the grocery store as she picked up the ingredients for her Thanksgiving meal. Everything was falling into place.

Muriel started the new year with a new job. She was able to enroll part-time. After six months in her current position, she would be eligible for reduced tuition. A year later, Muriel graduated with her Bachelor's degree and was eligible for a promotion.

Tuition Discount or Waiver
Many colleges and universities offer tuition discounts and tuition waivers to their employees, some offering this benefit to immediate family members as well. Check with each institution to find out what their policy is for your situation.

Certifications
Certifications show an employer that you have taken the initiative to learn more about a particular topic. Some certifications require an exam, others involve a passing score or grade of the subject matter, some require the payment of a fee, and others require membership in a professional association.

Research certifications in your field and find out if there is tuition assistance available as well as finding out if the certification will lead to additional promotion or compensation potential for you.

Free or Low-Cost Classes
If you need a quick resource to solve a problem or figure out how to do a task quickly, go online. The internet is chock full of resources:

www.youtube.com

www.udemy.com

www.teachable.com

www.craftsy.com

Tip: These are just a few options. Use the internet to find more.

Chapter Summary

Muriel was able to find a job which offered reduced tuition as a job benefit. With that benefit, she was able to complete her Bachelor's.

Muriel took advantage of those benefits to gain a certification and additional hours toward a Master's degree. She was also able to use the tuition discount for her children when they were ready for college.

Conclusion

Throughout this book, I have given you, the reader, a number of resources you can use to avoid taking out student loans and getting into debt.

So how did our students do? Let's get an update on each.

Alex finished all of his rehab. In his second year of college, he transferred to the university. He is continuing his studies in kinesiology. He has done very well in his classes landing on the Dean's List each semester. He continues his work at the sports facility, working more hours over the summer months to pay for school. He is also working as a coach to a team of four to six year olds in a youth soccer team. Both of his parents are working and his brother returned safely from his overseas deployment.

James finished his nursing training and earned his Bachelor of Science in Nursing. All of his children are in school. Emily was able to get a part-time job at the elementary school where the kids are attending, so she is able to have her days off whenever the children are out of school for holidays, breaks, and over the summer.

Muriel is so happy now that she has her Bachelor's degree. She has taken additional classes. She is able to support her family and is starting to help her kids with their college plans.

I know it is very expensive to go to college. College tuition increased at a rate of 179% at national universities. Out-of-state tuition increased a whopping 226%. Both of these figures are for increases over the last 20 years. (Mitchell, 2015)

Family dynamics and financial hurdles can make the decision to go to college very difficult. Adults in the Boomer generation are caring for their children as well as taking care of an elderly parent. There are plenty of resources to guide your decision.

Do your research and go to school debt-free.

References

American Kinesiology Association. (2015). *Careers in Kinesiology.* Champaign, IL: American Kinesiology Association.

Dumbauld, B. (2016). *Four Steps to Using Your Employer's Tuition Assistance Program.* Baltimore, MD: StraighterLine.

Gaisford, C. (2016). *Find Your Passion and Purpose; Four Easy Steps to Discover a Job you Want and Live the Life you Love.* Unknown: Blue Giraffe Publishing.

Hopkins, K. (2015). *11 Tuition-Free Colleges.* New York, NY: U.S. News and World Report.

Kelley, M. E. (2015). *Stay Safe on Campus.* Seattle, WA: Amazon Digital Services LLC.

Lobosco, K. (2016). *Americans are moving to Europe for free college degrees.* New York, NY: CNN Money.

Merriam-Webster Incorporated. (2015). *Simple Definition of Reciprocity.* Springfield, MA: Merriam-Webster Incorporated.

Mitchell, T. (2015). *Chart: See 20 Years of Tuition Growth at National Universities.* New York, NY: U. S. News and World Report.

Nasiripour, S. (2015). *The Federal Government Has No Idea How Much Americans Owe On Student Loans.* New York, NY: Huffington Post Politics.

National Association of Student Financial Aid Administrators. (2016). *State & Regional College Tuition Discounts.* Washington, DC: National Association of Student Financial Aid Admiinistrators.

Reed, D. C. (2015). *Project on Student Debt; State by State Data.* Oakland, CA and Washington, DC: The Institute for College Access and Success.

The College Board. (2016). The Basics on Grants and Scholarships. *The College Board*, New York, NY.

Thank you so much for reading my book.

I need to ask you a favor. Please leave a review. I really look forward to all your comments.

Thanks again.

Marcia E. Kelley

www.ingramcontent.com/pod-product-compliance
Lightning Source LLC
Chambersburg PA
CBHW061221180526
45170CB00003B/1099